INSCAPE
2016

Washburn University
Department of English
1700 SW College Ave
Topeka, KS 66621

Thanks to the Washburn University Department of English, and particularly to Thomas Fox Averill.

"the human work / of being greater than ourselves"

— Celia Gilbert

Vol. 41

inscapemagazine.org
facebook.com/inscapemagazine

Cover art: Detail from *Look*, by Kyra Miller
ink and watercolor, 24x32

Inscape, compiled annually at Washburn University in Topeka, Kansas, features poetry, fiction, nonfiction and visual art from the region and beyond.

INSCAPE
2016

CONTENTS

FICTION

NONFICTION

POETRY

ART

Editors' Choice

LOOK
Kyra Miller
ink and watercolor
24x32

Editors' Choice

WADE

Christopher Kuhl

Wade Farney awakes. It's 2:30 a.m. His parents and brother Lyle are asleep; the house is absolutely silent, so much so that his ears buzz. Is it the light? The previous day's echoes? Or is it the electrical currents in his "fidgety brain," as one of the gas station guys says? Whatever the case, the silence threatens him even as it soothes him with its (temporary) order.

Wade is famished. He didn't want dinner last night; his mother hovered over him until he finally ate three bites of pork chop. He knows she means well, but he feels smothered by her and oppressed by his father.

He gets up and goes to the kitchen, counting his steps as he goes. Twenty-three steps: a prime number. He opens the fridge; all he can find is leftovers, but some cheese too. He carefully slices eight pieces of mild cheddar. Then he takes some saltines out of the cupboard and, as carefully as he sliced the cheese, takes out eight crackers, trying not to break them, marveling at their fragility. But he breaks two, and he feels sorry for them; he hears them crying out and is sad. "Poor crackers, poor little crackers. I didn't mean to hurt you." He grieves silently for a moment and then, just as carefully, puts the six unbroken crackers back in their package, leaving just the broken crackers and the cheese to nibble. He carefully places the broken crackers in the trash and is left with just the cheese. Chaos, anxiety threaten. So he plans how to eat the cheese in an orderly manner. One nibble of cheese equals one-quarter of a slice of cheese. Four bites per slice, at eight slices, equals thirty-two bites. Thirty-two is a good number: each of its digits is a prime number. Order is restored. He no longer feels like crying.

But when he counts his way back to his bedroom, he gets twenty-six steps; the number isn't the same: why? And it's a bad number, divisible only by two or thirteen, both primes, but one unlucky. He feels threatened again. He wants to scream, and does so silently; his ears ring. Then he crawls under the covers, his blanket over his head, and takes some comfort in the ultimate darkness it affords. He tries to sleep.

Wade is twenty-three, same as the number of steps from his bedroom to the kitchen. He's been living with his parents, Amy and Winston Farney, ever since he dropped out of high school. He knows he shouldn't have; he should have finished and then gotten a job and his own place. But high school was chaotic, both in and between classes. And Wade felt invisible: people—students, teachers, administrators—didn't see him and walked all over him. And he had only one "sort of" friend, Stuart Marilley. They'd been in the same classes all their schooling lives, and Wade felt that Stuart was kind and understood about Wade's counting as he did things, and his attempt, when he did so, to find some livable order.

Stuart Marilley lived one road over and one field down from Wade's house, so, starting in third grade, they would sometimes walk together to school and back. Wade would count, timing his breaths and steps, trying to coordinate the two, and Stuart Marilley would talk. He knew Wade was talking and, in a weird sort of way, sharing in his own manner, too, and didn't press him for a more regular kind of conversation. Wade knew this, yet didn't know it, but he felt that Stuart Marilley was his best friend, if he could have such a thing. But he didn't tell anyone; it was a secret part of his life that his mother couldn't smother or his father oppress. And even though Stuart Marilley lived nearby, on the Tillman Road, Wade never invited him to his house; he couldn't fathom the chaos that bringing a stranger home would create. And he never went to Stuart Marilley's house: he didn't know his family and was frightened at the thought of being there with strangers whose ways he didn't know. Wade wondered if Stuart Marilley thought of him as a best friend. He had no way of knowing, and fearing more chaos and invisibility—ultimately to the whole world—he didn't ask. He loved Stuart Marilley and didn't want to lose him.

He loved Stuart Marilley as only young boys do before girls enter the picture or other boys and the tight camaraderie of sports teams come crashing in. Wade didn't do sports and, except in school or in the store with his mother, didn't see girls. They were incomprehensible, and they laughed at him—why?—and he was afraid and not interested, and felt hollow in their presence. His father had given him "the talk" when Wade was in the sixth grade, but it scared him, revolted him with its messiness and invasion of privacy and the need, his father said, to "take charge of, or at least respond to, the girl." Wade's father didn't realize the chaos he was suggesting, as though it were normal, and after all, "that's how your mother and I made you, son. So get out there and ride some ponies!"

After his father left, Wade cried silently, alone in the garage. Did Stuart Marilley know about this? What did he think about it? If Stuart Marilley started "riding some ponies," would Wade be invisible again? Would he, Wade Farney, still be Stuart Marilley's best friend? Or would Stuart Marilley drift away, abandoning Wade to what was becoming an increasingly unlivable world? Twenty-six divided by two equals thirteen.

Eighth grade. One day, on the way to school, Stuart Marilley was excited and proud. "I jerked off three times last night and it was great!" Wade didn't know exactly what he meant and didn't ask, but Stuart Marilley kept talking, and even mentioned a girl at school he'd like "to do it with." Wade was sick; he stopped, still counting just to keep breathing, and realized that what Stuart Marilley was talking about was what Wade's father had talked to him about in the garage. How could Stuart Marilley do this to him, or was Wade, even now, beginning to disappear again, becoming invisible even to Stuart Marilley? And then, sickened even more, he realized what the wet spots in his bed had been: part of his father's talk.

This was too much. He wanted to get away from Stuart Marilley and his dirty talk, and he dropped back, still counting but no longer listening to his friend. Wade had touched himself—sometimes it was necessary—but never the way his father had described to him "as he approached manhood." At least, anyway, as far as he knew, except maybe in his traumatizing dreams. And there were no signs of girls around, except in some faint, gauzy way. Was Wade invisible there, too?

Eighth grade was a difficult year for Wade generally: he felt increasingly misunderstood by his parents, and although he and Stuart Marilley continued to walk to school together, Wade began to feel that Stuart Marilley had other interests, and was not quite as into Wade as Wade was into him. This frightened Wade—the thought of losing his only friend (they still were friends, weren't they?). So he decided that, misunderstood or not, he would consult his brother Lyle, who, Wade knew from his silent observation, had many friends, both boys and girls, and was deeply involved in the ways of early manhood.

Wade cornered Lyle in the garage (the garage, of all places) before dinner, while his father was drinking a bourbon and water in the living room and reading the paper and his mother was in the kitchen, also enjoying a drink while she fixed dinner. Wade shuffled his feet.

"Uh, Lyle, how, um, how do you know if someone, if uh, someone likes you as much as, uh, you like them, I mean . . ." and Wade trailed off. He wasn't used to doing much talking that didn't involve counting, and he was afraid, maybe even terrified.

"You just hang around together, doing things, meeting their other friends, getting together, talking, watching TV at each other's houses. Stuff like that. If you're included, you're friends. Why?"

Wade was silently counting even as he listened. Lyle homed in. "Like, I know you're friends with Stuart, but you guys never do anything except walk to school together. That's not much of a friendship, if you ask me. You ought to have him over sometime and do something nonschool together."

Wade marveled at Lyle's virtuosity with words. Yes. Yes. Have Stuart Marilley over sometime. But what would they do? He began to have trouble breathing.

Lyle broke into Wade's thoughts. "Like maybe you could do some work on my car for me and see what develops. And there's girls, you know; you could talk about—"

Lyle stopped short. Wade's eyes were closed and he was whispering to himself. Lyle knew Wade had reached his conversational limit. "Just have him over. See how it goes." At that moment, Winston Farney came to the doorway and said, "Time's up, gentlemen. Dinner's ready." And he disappeared.

Wade pondered Lyle's words for weeks as he and Stuart Marilley went back and forth to school. Finally, in mid-spring, Wade and Stuart Marilley were walking home when Wade stopped short, took a deep breath, and, trying to be as smooth and calm as Lyle had been, directed some words to Stuart Marilley. "You wanna come over to my place today, uh, have a Coke?" First question; not bad. He tried again. "I could show you my brother's car he's working on. That might be kinda, uh, cool." Wade could go no further. He began to count the time until Stuart Marilley responded. "Yeah, sure. I'd like to see your brother's car. Got any music?"

This last question threw Wade off. Music? What music? He didn't listen to music, although he knew Lyle did. Well, maybe Lyle would lend him his transistor radio and they could listen to that. If Stuart Marilley wanted music, then he, Wade, his best friend, would give him music.

So Stuart Marilley walked with Wade to his house instead of splitting off on the Tillman Road to his own place. Wade was counting furiously, anxiously, almost skipping, almost stumbling. When they got to the house, they stood on the porch; Wade realized he needed to talk again. "You want a Coke? I think there's some in the fridge. You want a cold Coke? If there isn't any in the refrigerator, I can put ice in it. Do you like ice? I can—"

Lyle, who happened to be on the porch, said, "Shut up, Wade, and get the guy a Coke!" Stuart Marilley said, "Yeah, that'd be good."

Wade felt his eyes well up and fled to the kitchen, almost unable to count, he was so discombobulated, and got the Cokes, including one for Lyle.

When he got back to the porch, he found Lyle and Stuart Marilley deep in conversation about cars and girls. He couldn't speak, but just handed the Cokes around and sat, half-listening, counting, his ears ringing. Stuart Marilley was at his house, talking like an old friend to his brother, and they seemed perfectly at ease. Wade didn't know what to do; he couldn't talk about these things, but this apparently was what friends did. And what Stuart Marilley, his one and only friend, was doing. So Wade took a leap. "Lyle, can we see your car? I mean, if it's, uh, OK. We'll be careful, I promise." Lyle and Stuart Marilley looked at him, and Lyle said, "Sure, why not? You interested?" Stuart Marilley seemed genuinely interested. "OK. Cool." The three boys took their Cokes into the garage, where Lyle's Ford Fairlane sat, a work in progress. Lyle showed them around for a while, speaking car-talk, which Stuart Marilley seemed to follow but which was incomprehensible to Wade. Still, Stuart Marilley was at his house, talking to his brother, and this was what, according to Lyle, friends did. Wade, not much given to emotion, suddenly felt joy, utter and overwhelming joy and love. If he weren't so careful about things, he could have hugged not only his brother but Stuart Marilley too.

For a moment, he stopped counting and just breathed, admittedly panting a bit but living in the moment, in a numberless world. What was happening to him? Who was he? He had never thought about this before.

For the rest of the year, Stuart Marilley and Wade would hang out at his house two or three times a week, sometimes with, sometimes without Lyle. They'd drink Cokes, work on the car with Lyle's help, and listen to the Beatles and the Monkees on the radio. And Wade began to engage in snippets of conversation, which would interfere with his counting and frighten him a little. But Stuart Marilley seemed to intuit this (after all, they'd been schoolmates for years) and was gentle with Wade, responding to Wade's snippets and occasionally trying to have a short conversation. Eventually—it had to be; after all, they were about to start high school—the talk would come around to matters of manhood. Wade never started these conversations, Stuart Marilley did, and he didn't push Wade. He'd talk about a senior's muscles, or a cute girl, or who was going out with whom, and who'd "done it," and things he and Wade ought to do some time, "just for fun."

These conversations unnerved Wade; he knew this had to happen. Stuart Marilley was getting a little bored with doing the same old things, and he thought he ought to help get Wade out a little more, broaden his horizons. So one day Stuart Marilley invited Wade over to his house. Wade was hesitant but thought he could try. Maybe it would be OK; maybe no disaster would ensue. So he went.

And it was OK. They looked at the Marilley family cars; they played with the fishing tackle; they examined the hunting rifles in their cabinet in the garage. Slowly, over time, Wade got more comfortable. Yes, maybe they could go fishing at Chase's Lake. Yes, maybe they could go target shooting if Stuart Marilley's dad would take them.

And gradually the two friends seemed to be comfortable together: guys doing guy things back and forth between the two houses. Comfortable enough that Stuart Marilley could clap Wade on the shoulder over a joke, or touch his arm while showing Wade how to handle a rod and reel. Wade never returned the gestures, but he saw Stuart Marilley do it at school with the other guys, and even sometimes with a friendly girl, so Wade figured it was OK, even though the invasion of his space bothered him. But he could always regain his equilibrium by repeating sentences in his mind and counting the number of words. He didn't know if Stuart Marilley knew, but he didn't mind too much: the numbers were always there.

Then one day, while the boys were in the Marilley garage, Stuart Marilley was talking about kids at school and asked Wade if he'd ever kissed a girl. Wade, stunned, started reciting the prime numbers out loud, and Stuart Marilley knew he'd pushed Wade too far, even though he hadn't meant to. So he put his arm around Wade's shoulders and tried to reassure him: "It's OK, man, it's OK.

I didn't mean anything"—Wade was trembling all over now—"I mean, it's a big world with lots of girls and lots of time. You'll know when you're ready. Easy, big boy."

And Wade burst into tears. Slowly, Stuart Marilley got Wade, still crying, to sit down on one of the lawn chairs stored in the garage, and then, to distract him, to calm him down, took two rifles from the cabinet, one for Wade and one for himself. "Do you know how to clean a gun? These are beauties; I'll show you." So he got the cleaning oil, cloths, and rods, and the two boys, Stuart Marilley leading, worked. It was now silent in the garage except for clicks while cleaning and then, almost as an afterthought, loading them so, Stuart Marilley thought, they could ping some cans off the backyard fence, and settle Wade. As added comfort, Stuart Marilley offered some help. "You know, when you're getting ready to fire at a target, counting is really helpful as you go through the steps for aiming and firing."

Wade stopped, caught short and thankful: Stuart Marilley did understand him after all; yes, they were best friends. And, throwing all his phobias about personal space and touching aside, while holding the rifle down at his side, went to hug—yes, hug—Stuart Marilley. And even though they were boys, they were close. Wade leaned in—and Mr. Marilley came around the corner of the garage and roared, "What the hell are you guys doing?" Wade and Stuart Marilley jumped away from each other, Wade dropped the rifle, and it went off, hitting Stuart Marilley in the leg.

He would have kissed him. But now he'd never know.

Twenty-six divided by two is thirteen.

EMPIRE

Shannon Draper

for Shoichi Yokoi

By twenty-five, he could tell a man's inseam
without unrolling his tape. His small eyes,
silver-black, noted the heft of hipbones,
waist width, the elegant angle of ankles.

His Japan was not sword sharp, a knife blade
expertly pressed against an enemy throat,
a black robe full of precise and persistent
revenge, blousy with tradition.

By twenty-six, he was a soldier, measuring
steps instead of seams, dreaming of war
instead of shirtwaist dresses, a severed limb
encased in a perfect dolman sleeve.

His Japan was linen and silk, cotton and
tweed, dancers' skirts and grandfathers'
fine gold buttons marching up and down
bolts he touched each day with tender fingers.

By twenty-eight, he was in hiding, stitching
his silence into cave walls with torn nails,
his heart the red blood dot pulsing in the
Japanese flag, a button blinking back the darkness.

FLUENCY, INFUENCED

M. Trapp

Joan Didion's prose and I have a storied connection. When I was 15 I had read everything in sight. This wasn't hard to do in my house, as my parents never read at all, so there were no books at home, unless you count the four hardcovers always standing upright in the same spot next to the small yellow bud vase of dusty dried orange mums on the living room secretary desk: the *Family of Man* photography book, James Fixx's *The Complete Book of Running*, Gail Sheehy's *Passages*, and Wayne Dyer's *Your Erroneous Zones*. We were a self-help family with a yen for iconic photos, apparently. I had read all that my high school librarian had recommended (lots of Edna St. Vincent Millay, who, curiously, I have never heard anyone speak of again), and I had recently read all of Jane Austen and Charles Dickens on the recommendation of my friend Missy. I wandered the aisles of the only bookstore in my neighborhood, a Crown Books that carried lots of Danielle Steel. I knew I wanted something more, but I wouldn't have been able to tell you what that more was.

For my 16th birthday my dad and cousin took me on a surprise trip to San Francisco. On the flight there I was reading a music magazine that I had found at the airport bookstall. In it there was an interview with my then favorite musician: Lloyd Cole of Lloyd Cole and the Commotions. The interviewer asked him about his inspiration, and he said it was reading Joan Didion, that she was his favorite writer.[1] I had no idea who Joan Didion was, but I knew what I needed to read next. I picked up a paperback copy of *Play It As It Lays* at Cody's on Telegraph during that Bay Area trip.

I have a very clear memory of lying on my back in my bed once back at home in Newport Beach, spending a Saturday afternoon reading the entire book at once. I remember thinking that I really didn't get what I was reading, but I wanted to keep going. I soon read *The White Album* and *Slouching Toward Bethlehem.* I was still a little lost, but I kept on reading. It turned out that *Run River,* the next book I read, was what really got me hooked. I read and reread that book for years.

For reasons that are still unclear to me, I gave my mom a hardback copy of *Democracy* for Christmas when I was a junior in high school, after my parents had divorced and I was living with my dad. My mom was, and is, a woman who has never to my knowledge even read the newspaper all the way through, yet I was quite excited to give her the book. A naive hope that she would become a reader? That we would finally have something in common? That I would seem as sophisticated as I wanted to feel? That she would like me? That I would like her?

That book, ever unread, became a fixture on her sofa table. It was practically a piece of furniture. The dustjacket had fade marks that corresponded exactly to the little blue and green cloisonné box she kept on top of it for years.

I found myself alone in my mom's living room recently and decided she was never worthy of such a gift; I slipped the book into my bag and took it back with me to Seattle. She never missed it, as far as I can tell.

That I was alone in my mom's living room at all says much about me and my mom. We are rarely together. I feel she doesn't want me around. Who knows how she feels. I used to want to know; now I just want to avoid the whole thing. On that trip I brought my toddler daughter, my first child. My husband and I and our little girl, Violet, live in Seattle. My mom, who lived in Newport

---

[1] While double checking my facts for this essay, wanting to see if I could find the now-ancient Lloyd Cole interview I read those many years ago, I discovered that Dave Eggers also once read a similar (or the same?) interview, and he credits this with initiating him into a lifelong love of Didion. Darn! My own story is once again told before I had the chance to tell it!

Beach, rarely saw us. I came down to Orange County with Violet to be at my Aunt Lori's surprise 50th birthday party. My husband stayed in Seattle to work.

My mom called me before I left Seattle. She sounded excited to have me down. It felt like a new chapter. Maybe it takes having a granddaughter to make my mom want to connect, I thought. Surprisingly, she insisted that I stay at her place when I was in California. I was 35 and had lived away from home since I was 17. Never on my visits home in all those years had my mom offered me a place to stay. I always stayed at my dad's. I thought it was a given. My mom had her new, single life. Her place was immaculate, unwelcoming. But here she was offering me and Violet a place to stay.

I'm always a sucker for new beginnings, so I took her up on the offer.

I got to Orange County. My mom had sent her new boyfriend, Bob Hawkins, to pick me up at the airport. I had never met him before. He seemed nice enough. It was unclear to me why my mom couldn't make it to the airport herself. Bob said something about her car not being big enough for Violet's car seat.

Bob let me into my mom's place, and he told me to make myself at home. My mom was at his place, he said. He lived closer to my Aunt Lori's, so he said they would both stay there to be ready to help with the big party. He said they'd see me tomorrow night at Lori's. Then he left.

I was alone, with Violet, in my mom's place. Yes, I could stay in her home, but she wouldn't be there. So weird, and yet so predictable.

The living room was freezing. I turned up the heat. I went to the kitchen and opened the fridge. There was some quince jam, a few baby carrots, and a carton of soy milk. Gross. It was like she didn't even live here anymore. She must be spending all her time with Bob Hawkins. Violet and I made do with the Cliff Bar and some Cheerios I had in my bag for dinner that night. I was pissed and hurt.

I made my way to the bedroom. It was the most unwelcoming place you can imagine. And certainly not child friendly at all with her pristine, perfectly white duvet cover and all the expensive Apple products and cords on every flat surface. What the hell was she thinking inviting me here? My first feeling was rage. But then I reverted to my old high school babysitting ways. If no one else was here, what a perfect time to snoop. Maybe I'd find some old diaries or letters, some telling to-do lists—anything to give me even the tiniest bit of insight into this person who was, by all accounts, my mother.

But even her personal stuff lacked personality. Everything was tidy to a fault. It was like I was sitting in one of those model homes in the planned community of Irvine that we used to walk through when I was little and my parents were looking for rental properties to buy. My mom's bedroom felt like a staged room. I found zero personal effects.

I went back into her living room, and there it was, her old copy of *Democracy.* It looked like she hadn't opened it since I had given it to her in December of 1986, if she had even opened it then. Fuck it, I thought. I am normally pretty sentimental about gifts. No matter what someone gives me, even if it is the most un-me thing I can think of, I never return or exchange it. I hold on to everything, especially the idea that someone cared enough, however ill-advisedly, to get a gift. But I was mad that night. Who cares that the book had been a gift. The receiver of this gift was clearly not interested. I put Violet to sleep in the white, frigid bedroom, and to keep her warm I got into bed alongside her. But first I made sure to stuff my mom's unread hardcover copy of *Democracy* deep into my travel bag, under all the diapers and onesies and board books. I added it to my Didion shelf in my book collection in Seattle, where it still sits nicely today.

When I was finally a senior in college at Berkeley, I was deciding what to write for my honors thesis. I had just spent three years reading writers like Wordsworth and Pope and Shakespeare and Hawthorne and Eliot and Spenser and Melville. Our honors thesis instructor told us that since the thesis would be a year-long project, we should write on something we really loved. I thought immediately of Didion. A few weeks later, my friend and roommate and academic idol Michael asked me what I planned to write my thesis on. I said Joan Didion. We were having Thai food for lunch at Racha Cafe on Telegraph. Michael had introduced me to Thai iced tea the year before when I was a junior, and I was hooked.

I remember his words exactly: "Really? Didion? Kind of a thin choice, don't you think? By her own admission she got a C in a writing course at Berkeley when she was here. I don't think there's enough to her for you to take her seriously."

I was impressionable and insecure; I immediately backed off from my first choice. What did I know? My family talked about passing the chips at the dinner table, while Michael had regaled me with tales of his family debating for hours at the table about something they'd all heard together on NPR. I don't think my family knew what NPR was. I wanted desperately to be smart enough to be friends with people like Michael. That year I ended up writing about Virginia Woolf's *The Waves*—a fascinating novel, but it was no *Run River*.

After my honors thesis, I went to grad school in English at Berkeley in 1996, where we read lots of Foucault and Benjamin and Gramsci and Althusser. I felt severely underread, out of my league, out of my element. And so began my long hiatus from Joan Didion's prose.

I read *The Year of Magical Thinking* pretty much the minute it came out in 2005. At the time, my oldest daughter was a newborn. She nursed seemingly all the time, and she would only sleep with me by her side. I had to sneak out of bed at night, trying my hardest not to wake her with any little mattress groans or floorboard creaks. I grabbed a tiny reading light, propped myself up on the floor next to and nearly under her bed, and read Didion's newest book in the dark, small hours of the morning, hoping to get as many pages in as I could before my baby woke up and needed me. What I recall most about reading the book that time was that I was resentful. I was happy to have a baby. I wanted a daughter. But I was also lonely. I was up at all kinds of odd hours nursing the baby while my husband slept. My dissertation was on hold indefinitely, and I felt alone sneaking in this one little pleasure of reading Joan Didion's latest book before someone in the house needed me for something or other. In my then-fragile state of mind, the book seemed very much about an idyllic marriage and an even more idyllic mother-daughter connection. I felt mad and jealous as I read. My life in comparison to Didion's (albeit a life she was mourning the loss of) felt small, prosaic, stunted. The book made me feel diminished. Poor me, I thought. My daughter is so needy, and my husband works too much away from home.

The things I most recalled from the book after that first reading were Didion and her husband writing all day, then swimming together in their Los Angeles pool every afternoon. I recalled episodes of making soufflés, and of her needing to talk to her husband about everything and anything. I recalled her writing about how when she was in shock after he died, her first thought was always, go to the literature, read up on this, learn to articulate it. What struck me most was that she and her husband were a great match, and that she saw the world through writing and reading. It was a hard book to read—both because obviously it was about a hard topic, loss, but also because in its grief the book was really about a love and connection that felt very rare, and I am an envious person.

I read the book again this month. Clearly, I had given it short shrift last time around. I was in no state of mind to read a book about love and loss when I was, as I can see now, still reeling from giving birth and learning to love this new, foreign-for-me life of family and marriage and parenting. It was hard to read about real, true love and loss when my own family connections often felt so tenuous and slapdash. Where Didion writes about what seems like a version of marital and parental love that was meant to be, that was always deep and perfectly formed, my own life and loves by comparison often feel haphazard, accidental, and hard-won to me.

The book this time spoke to me on many levels. And I feel happy to be able to write about Didion after all these years, after Michael in Berkeley and academia in general pretty much convinced me that what I loved to read was "thin." Didion's prose is anything but thin, and *The Year of Magical Thinking* is a complex and compelling glimpse into how we love and how we grieve.

This is a book about connection, about how we tell or don't tell trauma, about how we understand and communicate loss. Didion writes of the immediate period after her husband John's sudden death,

> This is my attempt to make sense of the period that followed, weeks and then months that cut loose any fixed idea I had ever had about death, about illness, about probability and luck, about good fortune and bad, about marriage and children and memory, about grief, about the ways in which people do and do not deal with the fact that life ends, about the shallowness of sanity, about life itself. I have been a writer my entire life. As a writer, even as a child, long before what I wrote began to be published, I developed a sense that meaning itself was resident in the rhythms of words and sentences and paragraphs, a technique for withholding whatever it was I thought or believed behind an increasingly impenetrable polish. The way I write is who I am, or have become, yet this is a case in which I wish I had instead of words and their rhythms a cutting room, equipped with an Avid, a digital editing system on which I could touch a key and collapse the sequence of time, show you simultaneously all the frames of memory that come to me now, let you pick the takes, the marginally different expressions, the variant readings of the same lines. This is a case in which I need more than words to find the meaning. This is a case in which I need whatever it is I think or believe to be penetrable, if only for myself.

Words are powerful, and words are obscure. They both reveal and disguise feeling. Here Didion points to the inadequacy of language in the face of love and loss, the smallness of story when it comes to capturing life. She writes of how difficult it is to tell your own story. There are so many memories and feelings, so many events, that it feels impossible to order them into any sort of coherent narrative. In her mind, they all play together, at once, and the best way to capture them is to dispense with words and pacing and plot and to simply let the reader in on her grief and memories as if they are watching it all live or on film. Didion lets us know here that she feels, even as a writer, that words inevitably fall short. Yet all the while her characteristically balanced, concise, and beautiful prose is so moving, so evocative. She tells us that, even as a writer, she can't find the phrasing to match her feelings, yet, even if it only gets us there halfway, this is enough for me. I was moved.

The passage above in particular, as well as the book as a whole (and its successor, *Blue Nights*, which I also read right after it came out (and which I also had both uncomfortable and overwhelming feelings about)), is a perfect example for me of how to write in the essay form, how to write about your own life without being maudlin, how to analyze and probe your own character in a clean, clear prose voice.

I have two daughters now, and after eight more years of parenting and being married, when I read *The Year of Magical Thinking* this second time, it felt true and right. Didion's marriage and her connection to her daughter were indeed powerful, and I can see why one might, why I might, be envious of these things. But I've learned to relax more into my own life, and it gives me pleasure to read this time around all that Didion felt and thought. I learned something, many things, about love and connection in this book. I also learned what it means to face hard truths with grace, and how impossible things can be said so well.

I love Joan Didion's writing. I love the way she can say so much while seeming to say so little. This is not thinness. It's a beautiful restraint, and I aspire to it.

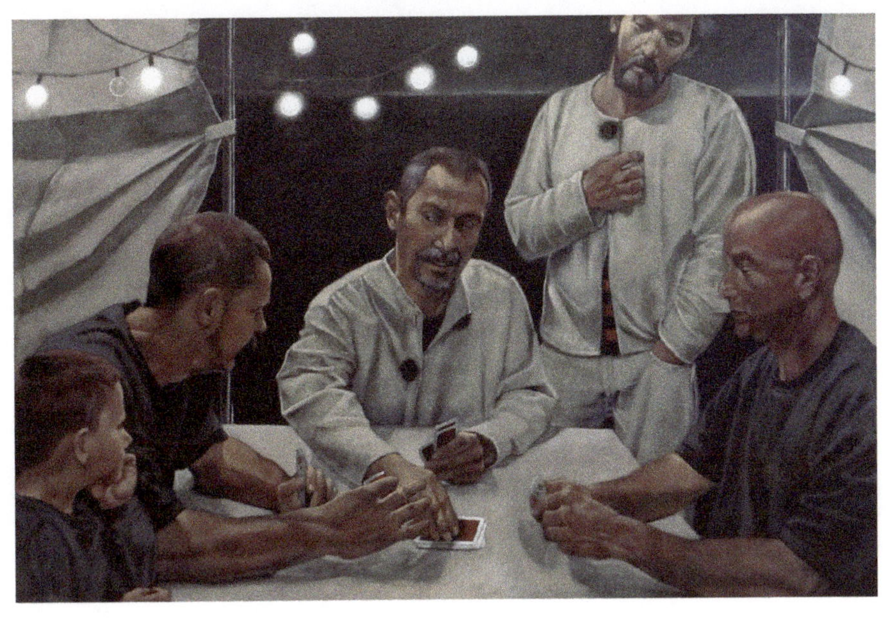

THE CARD PLAYERS
Barbara Waterman-Peters
oil on canvas
24x36

A FROG IN BOILING WATER

Dallas Woodburn

3642 Maplewood Drive is a three-story flagstone house with a gabled roof and four-car garage, nestled deep within the protective arms of Red Fern Ranch, which is not a ranch at all but rather a gated community in a northern California suburb not much nuisanced by crime to begin with. In this neighborhood, the houses preen. Windows sparkle. The sidewalks are dutifully swept; the curbs are free of debris; parked cars do not clutter the streets. If one's lawn ventures into unkempt neglect, the Homeowner's Association sends a firm-but-gentle reminder by way of a firm-but-gentle fine. At 3642 Maplewood Drive, gardeners come every Wednesday morning to trim the hedges, mow the lawn, rake the leaves.

A family lives here. A mother, a father, and a son.

I am born at 3642 Maplewood Drive at 8:53 p.m. on a Friday night. Not a soul in Red Fern Ranch knows about me. It is a dry, still night, static electricity palpable in the air. I am born in the attic.

*

On this Friday night, minutes after my birth, an argument simmers in the ornately tiled kitchen. The son—Jason, a high school senior, admitted to Berkeley next fall—wants to go out with his friends. But his mother is adamantly against him going anywhere.

"I just have a feeling," she says. "A bad feeling. I can't explain it."

Jason looks down at the granite countertop, silently runs his finger along the grout between the tiles.

"Please, honey. Stay here tonight, will you? Safe and sound."

"I'll be safe, Mom. I promise."

"Honey—"

"I won't even be out that late."

The father stamps into the kitchen and bangs cabinets, opening and closing them at random. He settles upon a bag of trail mix, which he pours into his palm. "Listen to your mother," he says, using his no-arguing voice.

"I promise I won't be out late."

"Jason, what have we talked about?"

The son sighs. "Fine. I'll be a loser with no social life."

The mother's face relaxes. She had felt tears welling up inside her, but she was able to tamp them down before an outburst overtook all thought. She smiles gratefully at George, reaches over and strokes Jason's hair. For a few moments, he stands there and lets her.

"Thank you," she says—to George, to Jason, to them both.

It is 9:02 p.m.

*

We cannot choose the circumstances in which we are born. Once I am sparked to life, a single thought drives my existence: consume.

All I know is, I am ravenous. I cannot stop myself.

*

Jason ducks away from his mother and heads up to his bedroom.

"There's a movie on HBO tonight you might like!" his father calls after him. "Some apocalypse action movie."

No response, other than the clomping of Jason's tennis shoes on the stairs.

George looks at Marie and shrugs. She shrugs in return, giving him a playful smile before turning away, her attention snagged by the sinkful of dirty dishes. She is wearing a long skirt that clings to her hips. Her hair, dyed a dark brown, gleams in the warm kitchen light. George is swept by the feeling of how it used to be—the two of them, together, apart from everyone else.

It is this feeling that spurs him across the kitchen, wiping the peanut crumbs off his palms. Marie is bent over the big kitchen sink, arms in sudsy water, rinsing pasta sauce off dinner plates and dressing out of salad bowls. George watches her shadowy reflection in the darkened kitchen window, her eyes cast downward, absorbed in her task. The steamy water fills the sink, a continuous rushing sound. He stands behind her, inching closer, closer, and then he's pressed to her, wrapping his arms around her waist, kissing her soft neck.

She flinches, her body stiffening. George pulls away. She turns the water off and flicks her hands once, twice, three times. When she turns, finally, her expression reminds George of a frightened animal—of the squirrel they found one summer, trapped in the attic, desperate to find a way out.

"I'm sorry," she says. "It's just—I've told you—it's hard for me, right now. Being touched."

George takes another step away from her. He runs his hand over his thinning hair, back, forward, back.

"It's not you," she says. "It's not anything to do with you."

"It feels that way, though."

"It's not, I swear. I love you. I'm just—I'm not there yet."

But will you ever get there? George wants to ask. *Will you ever be my wife again?* Eight months since they've made love. Two months since her last breakdown, when the doctor put her on that new medication.

"It's just that you've seemed better lately," he says. "I thought I could kiss you without—frightening you away."

"It's not you, George."

"I guess I was mistaken. Sorry." He raps his knuckles twice on the countertop. His smile is forced, worse than a frown. "I'll be upstairs in my study," he says. He works as a financial planner for small businesses. "Got some emails to send."

Marie nods and turns back to the dishes. The water is scalding, but she doesn't turn it colder. She watches her hands, scrubbing the delicate china. She watches them as if they are someone else's hands. Her skin is a bright pink. *Maybe*, she thinks. *Maybe tonight. Maybe I can try to stand it.*

It is 9:14 p.m.

*

Once you are alive, it is impossible to know what it was like before life. Yet I can taste memories all around me. This cluttered attic is drowning in memories. Christmas tinsel caught around a popsicle-stick ornament. A Kodak Instamatic with half a roll of unused film inside. A child's rocking chair carved from redwood, a delicacy.

I devour the memories, and then they disappear and I am left famished, raging for more. I am suffocating. I need oxygen. I need to breathe.

*

Jason flops backwards onto his bed, feeling suffocated in the emptiness of his bedroom, the vast hardwood floors stretching around him like a wasteland. He wants to be in a small room crowded with noise and people. He wants a stranger to spill a drink on his shoes; he wants a girl to sob into his shoulder. He wants to dance in the crushing sweaty heart of a San Francisco club. He wants to stumble out onto a darkened street and have no idea where he is what time it is or how he got there, and not care. He wants to be reckless, to dare life: *C'mon, send me the best you've got. I'm ready.*

His cell phone buzzes. Jason ignores it, knowing it's Danny or Steve or Brenden, one of the guys, wanting to know what time he'll be there tonight. If their parents give them a hard time about going out, they go anyway. Or they sneak out later, or they lie about where they're going. Jason has never been able to lie. His face burns and his words run together. And it's gotten worse since his mother's last episode. She's always been an anxious person, fluttery and hands-wringy, moved to tears by burnt breakfast toast, but Jason never thought he would see her like that. Curled into a ball on the floor of her walk-in closet, her eyes huge and far away. Rocking back and forth, back and forth, in a slow terrifying mechanical way. The doctors later referred to it as a panic attack, and she has been back to normal since then, her medication living calmly in the kitchen cupboard alongside the multivitamins and Tums. But Jason can't shake the image of her, wild-eyed and quivering, and he worries that any little thing could send her reeling back to that dark place. And what if the next time, she doesn't recover? What if her small yellow pills no longer work? What then?

His phone buzzes again. Jason pushes himself off his bed and reaches for it. Brenden.

"So what time you want me to pick you up?"

"I don't know," Jason says. "I don't know if I'm going."

"Dude, don't bail out now. You always bail."

"It's just … you know how strict my parents are."

"So sneak out. It's not a big deal. Listen, I'll pick you up at the corner across from the movie theater."

"I'll try."

"Quit this 'trying' bullshit, just be there at 10. Okay? Your parents will be asleep by then anyway. They'll never know the difference."

"Better make it 10:30," Jason says.

"Sure, 10:30. But seriously, don't bail on me, alright? I'm doing this for you."

"I know." Jason's social standing has nosedived the past few months. He's declined so many invitations that he's fading into anonymity. Brenden, his best friend since sixth grade, confided that people think he's stuck up about getting into Berkeley. Brenden's a good friend. He wants to help.

"Thanks, man," Jason adds, feeling a surge of gratitude. "I'll be there." But Brenden's already hung up.

*

I am half an hour old, working my way through the boxes of old EPs, Halloween costumes, baby clothes. The life-size papier-mâché sculpture Jason made of Abraham Lincoln in sixth grade. The chest of wool sweaters no one has worn since the Reagan years, mothballed and delicious.

*

Before, when Marie heard the word "breakdown," she associated it with a sudden shift—something triggered. Like a twig stepped on by a heavy boot, snapped cleanly in two. Before: whole. After: broken. But Marie's breakdown was not like that. For her, the breakdown was something that built over a matter of days and weeks and months, a gradually increasing sense of claustrophobia—compounded by guilt that she was feeling anything but gratitude for her life. Because, Marie knew, she had much to be grateful for: a loving husband, a good son, a beautiful home in a safe neighborhood. Lunches with friends at the Country Club and volunteer work at the library. She never worried about money. She and George rarely argued. She had a life people yearned for and envied. An easy life.

Maybe, she thought at first, her anxiety stemmed from Jason—the knowledge that he would be leaving them soon; moving out of the house and off to college, away to the next stage of his life, independent from them. He would not need her any longer. She felt purposeless, restless. And part of it was related to Jason, yes—but, if she was honest with herself, it had been a while since he had needed her, *really* needed her. Moving out was the final step of a process long begun.

As the weeks dragged on, the feeling within her expanded, and it was bigger than Jason, bigger than George, bigger than menopause or the onset of winter, the bare-limbed trees like ghosts in the yard. She went for long walks through the neighborhood, wanting to just keep walking, away, away, away from it all. Wanting to burn everything down and start again. Renewal in having nothing. Freedom in the ashes of what used to be.

Marie heard once that if you put a frog in a pot of water that is ever-so-slowly brought to a boil, the frog will not notice the increase in temperature, and will be boiled alive without even trying to leap from the pot. Her breakdown happened when she noticed. Her breakdown was an attempt at a leap.

*

I bide my time, keeping quiet, gaining ground without much notice.

It is 9:32 p.m.

*

Marie lifts her knuckle to Jason's bedroom door and tentatively knocks.

"Come in."

The door whines as she opens it. Jason is flopped back on his bed, spiral notebook on his bent knees, the bedside lamp blazing a halo of light on his face.

"What are you working on?" she asks from the doorway.

"Homework. Thought I'd get something done since I'm not going anywhere."

Sometimes, when she looks at her son, Marie is amazed by how strange he seems to her. How unknowable. For nine long months, he grew inside her—she was his everything—and now. Now he humors her? Resents her? Now they are strangers who just happen to live under the same roof.

"Thank you for staying in tonight," she says.

"It's no big deal."

"I just have a bad feeling. A mother's intuition. I know you think I'm crazy ..."

Marie trails off, but Jason doesn't respond. She waits a moment more, then says, "I'm going over to Safeway, to get groceries for the week."

"You're going *now*?" Jason sits up. "Is the store even open this late?"

"Till eleven. I hate to deal with the crowds."

"How long will you be gone?"

"Not long. Anything you want me to get for you?"

Jason leans back against his pillow. "Mountain Dew."

"Okay," Marie says, not even putting up a fight about the amount of sugar or chemicals in that drink, his favorite since he was a boy. She understands that Jason is bargaining with her. He is staying home tonight, and she is buying him Mountain Dew. She can do that.

"I love you," she says, and shuts the door before he can decline to say it back.

*

I am spurred onward by desire, not love. Need, not want. There is a difference. I do not love anything. I do not know what it means to be selfless. Yet there is honor in my pursuit: I am exactly where I am supposed to be, doing exactly what I am supposed to do. Consumption is my life's purpose. It must be. If not, why would it be such an irrepressible urge within me?

*

George is down the hall in his study, doing online Sudoku. Marie comes in without knocking.

"I'm going to the store," she says.

Ever since her last breakdown, she's been going to the store late at night, when no one else is there. George thought it would be good for them to shop together, or for her to go during the day or evening like everyone else, when she would have a chance to run into friends. He hates to see her withdrawing from the world like this—so scared, so on edge. But her doctor, a thick-haired pompous wearer of sweater-vests whom George does not trust, sided with Marie, saying it would be best for her to avoid crowds and "anxiety-inducing situations."

"Okay," George says now, not looking up from his computer screen. "Drive safe."

"I will. See you in a little while."

"I'll probably be asleep when you get back. I'm thinking of hitting the sack soon."

"Oh. Okay, then." The hurt on her face is what George wanted, yet it brings him no satisfaction. Is this what they've come to—round after round of bruised feelings and subtle barbs?

"It's been a long week," he adds.

Marie nods, then leaves, shutting the door behind her. George closes Sudoku and opens his favorite porn site.

It is 9:43 p.m.

*

I can detect life in the layers of house below me, creaking the floorboards, rattling the pipes. But they do not frighten me. They have no idea I am here. No idea how strong I am becoming with every passing second.

Somewhere in this attic is a box that has not been opened in twenty-six years. Inside rests a wedding dress, carefully folded and wrapped in tissue paper. It is the last thing I find before everything comes crashing down.

*

Jason stares at his bedroom ceiling, wondering what he'll tell his parents if he gets caught tonight.

George watches the pixilated gyrating blondes, trying to fight away the image of his wife's timid, broken eyes.

Marie climbs into her Lexus with her reusable grocery bags and backs down the driveway, thinking how monstrous the house looks at night, like a dark palace against the blue-black sky. Like something out of a grim fairy tale.

It is 9:53 p.m.

*

In the ensuing weeks, at George's and Jason's funerals, people will try to console Marie with words, facts, scientific terms. It was an electrical fire. It started in the attic. There is no way anyone could have known. It was a slow-burning, smoldering nightmare. No warning. No smoke. The ceiling just collapsed, and by then it was too late.

Nobody's fault. Just one of those bizarre freak accidents.

But Marie does not believe in accidents. Until the day she dies (June 16, four years later, her Lexus colliding head-on into a tree) she is convinced the fire is her fault. She is the reason it came into being. She is the one who left; who abandoned it all, everything, to burn.

*

It is 10:36 on Friday night. The back seat of Marie's Lexus bulges with groceries. She can see the smoke from all the way down Maplewood Drive. She presses her foot to the gas pedal, hurrying, hurrying, her heartbeat a blur of thumping. As if a part of her knows what she will find.

Fire trucks, an ambulance, neighbors crowding the street. The choking smell of soot and ashes.

3642 Maplewood Drive, engulfed in flames.

*

Our lives are short. That is the nature of any existence. I know I will die before I am ready—but, then again, won't we all?

The men lift their hoses and gun me down.

SAMPLER: BETRAYAL

Lee Varon

for my mother and grandmother

You've pitched your tents
in my blood and I want you gone.
No longer a fragile thing who dents
when brushed or bruised, I've drawn

a different course from you.
I wouldn't seek it
though I can withstand betrayals. True,
you gave me the split

bullet in grandfather's brain
but half that shot passed through
as I passed through your pain
to the place where love drew

a picture and the dead
are at peace. Where goldwork trims
everything and in the thread
of a needle love spins.

BETWEEN BOURBON AND ERROR

Zac Walsh

Perhaps love is knowing life can never be long enough
now, that every rift will tire you less than this
tending.

Love could be remembering how much you wanted to
die, young days brought to the fore when living was simply
getting.

Mania may be a form of love, a word the Greeks forgot or
knew, but never wanted to take as seriously as the cause of such
thinking.

Pain is to know the first walk in the garden must
happen, so that the second face would be worth
finding.

Comfort has no place in this world if you care to be
alive, yet the was is for now a way to rest before you allow
regretting.

Tomorrow is no dream and no idea that will allow itself to be
refused, as the rest flows into the pond same as the
mending.

Wounds show slow and heal in our steps faster than our
thoughts, this gash all we can do is savor, as what we call
    done is tuned to
becoming.

IN THE UNMADE WE SEE THE WORLD

Susan Rich

In the half-finished remodel
dangle rows of fraying knob and tube,

the walls show bare wood, skeletal
renditions of dust—

On the notebook's open page:

a few incomprehensible lines,
first draft of a fable or a song.

A stretched canvas, perfectly blank
for the painter's next addition,

or the tailor and her cloth; it's a kind
of partnership until it's not

not yet wedding dress, not yet culottes.

In the not-yet-made we see the next
president and the palm reader.

In the unmade world are green things—

promise of a cotyledon or the cream bud
of a honeycrisp, her grafted blue ribbon tree.

THE LIMITS OF ROSIN

Susana H. Case

It's hard to imagine that liquid
from a conifer can be used to create
both violin music and wine and flux
to solder metals. And after my labors,
I can put on a frilly red dress, rub
a powder made from pine on my heels
in order not to slide when dancing.
Or, pull out my sword, do the same
to strut my stuff when fencing.

Because anything versatile is volatile.
Because anything volatile is capable
of flight. Colophony: hard, brittle,
translucent. Take a little rosin,
mix it with wax and oil and friction
and poof!—I'm a magician—
mystic smoke from my fingertips,

though I can't stop the losses;
even when gunked,
my fingers let so much slip through.

OTHER PEOPLE/OTHER PEOPLE'S LAND
Reineke Hollander
mixed media (oil, canvas, textiles, sewing, photograph)
60x35

BRAIDS AND TANGLES

Enid Kassner

I climb the stairs to the second floor, dark oak creaking. Quietly, I make my way to the largest of the three bedrooms. The hardwood floors are covered in a sheet of linoleum, its swirling pale pink pattern designed to resemble carpeting. The room's windows look out to the street, and an old mahogany vanity rests in an alcove. Dust motes dance in the angled path of sun spilling onto its surface. Sliding open a drawer, I find the treasure I'm seeking: a small, worn, cardboard box, its flowered pattern faded. Perhaps it once held fancy soap or an embroidered handkerchief. I lift off the top and turn its tissue-wrapped contents into my small, seven-year-old hands. Two heavy coils of curly chestnut hair, tied at each end with strings: my Aunt Ruthie's childhood braids.

*

When I was young, my family drove nearly every weekend from our home in Milwaukee to my maternal grandparents' house in Burlington, Wisconsin—a seemingly endless forty-mile ride. Some combination of cousins, aunts, and uncles would gather there, consuming kosher dairy lunches at the kitchen table—always with hefty slices of my grandmother's home-baked bread. If I was lucky, my cousin Miriam would also be there. She and I were the only girls of our generation: outnumbered three-to-one by boy cousins.

We spent hours playing outside, climbing the sour cherry trees in the back yard and picking the tart fruit for my grandmother's delicious pie. Or we walked by ourselves to the corner store for penny candy.

Indoors, we knew which rooms were off-limits, but we were free to explore the basement, with its fruit cellar and "junk drawer" full of random gadgets. It was a treat to go upstairs when one of the older cousins pulled the chain to a ceiling door. The door brought down a staircase that led to an enormous attic, where my uncles' World War II uniforms—one Army, the other Navy—hung from the rafters. But Miriam and I mostly played in the bedroom that our mothers (along with Aunt Ruthie and another sister) had shared as children.

We found mysterious remnants from their childhoods: old school primers; an illustrated book of nursery rhymes, its cover long gone; speckled clay marbles; and a folding yardstick with smooth metal hinges. There were red and gold SWEE-TOUCH-NEE Tea tins ("The Aristocrat of Teas") with their treasure chest design and hinged tops. Inside the tins were tiny charms made of black metal or creamy plastic: a billy goat, a woman diver, a Scottie dog, a teensy pair of binoculars. The most ancient tea can bore Cyrillic letters, a hint of my immigrant grandfather's Russian origins. There were button boxes, embroidery hoops and threads, thimbles and needle cases, wooden or ivory dice, clunky old silver jacks, mismatched sets of checkers and chess. But most fascinating, to me, were my Aunt Ruthie's braids.

I was familiar with a faded black-and-white photograph of Ruthie as a girl. Two plump braids fell over her shoulders onto a flowered cotton dress as she stood, skinny legs together, in white anklets and sturdy lace-up shoes. A smile crinkled the corners of her eyes, which were fringed with dark, curly lashes. When Ruthie was thirteen, the braids were cut to make way for a more grown-up hairdo.

I loved to hold the glossy braids and rub their softness against my cheek. They testified to Ruthie's cherished place in the family. Of all the children, only her tresses had been saved.

*

Ruthie was the baby—the last of my grandmother's eight children, of whom only six survived to adulthood. The oldest two had already died by the time Ruthie came along in 1930. She was the pampered baby girl of a large family: the sweetest and the prettiest. Even when the relatives gossiped about each other, no one had anything bad to say about Ruthie.

In her twenties, Ruthie and her husband, Hal, had three boys, but she suffered many miscarriages trying to have a fourth: the hoped-for girl. She never succeeded, so she treated Miriam and me like daughters. Because Miriam and her brother lived in Madison, I was often the lone girl among boys at my Milwaukee cousins' birthday parties. Ruthie always baked a foot-tall angel food cake, amply iced, with a fancy sugar medallion over the center hole.

At every party, Ruthie gave me the coveted sugar disk. I didn't even like the hard, overly sweet candy, but in my childish, egocentric view of the world, it felt right that I, the only girl, should get preferential treatment. I was in my fifties before I learned that my cousins still resented me for stealing what they considered their rightful birthday prize. Looking back now, it seems strange that the birthday boy wasn't the one to get the treat.

But I loved the way Ruthie made me feel special. She had saved dolls and porcelain tea sets from her childhood and gave them to me when I was the right age to play with them. She was always gentle. Her family seemed happy, perfect—at least in contrast to my own, in which my father had an explosive temper, my mother was depressed, and my brother and I fought. I sometimes wished I could live with Aunt Ruthie and Uncle Hal.

*

I moved from Wisconsin to Washington, D.C., after finishing college. Over the four decades that followed, I returned to see family only once or twice a year. Like everyone, I was busy with work, my immediate family or friends, and other activities that always seemed more pressing. I relied mostly on reports from my mother or Miriam to get family news.

About eight years ago, my mom complained that Ruthie's memory was terrible. I didn't pay much attention to her. Ruthie was then only seventy-four. She had practiced Transcendental Meditation (TM) for more than thirty years. She ate everything organic. She exercised. Surely nothing was wrong.

But on my next visit home, a few months after the phone call with my mom, I understood her concerns. The extended family had gathered at Ruthie and Hal's for dinner. While Ruthie was as sweet and smiley as ever, I noticed that she repeated the same question every few minutes, just as happy to receive the unvarying answer each time. Plaques and tangles were twisting through her brain, eating away at healthy tissue, slowly but steadily. Nobody wanted to talk about what was happening or how serious it was.

As the years progressed, she eventually was diagnosed with Alzheimer's disease. Still, Ruthie's cheerful demeanor remained even as she lost the ability to prepare meals, to speak more than occasionally, to walk, to move unassisted, and, sometimes, even to swallow. Her youngest son told me that one day, after he'd called her "mom," she replied, "I'm not who you think I am."

Always tiny, Ruthie seemed to shrink to the size of a child. Her eyes still sparkled as they did in the photograph of her with the long braids. Hal wouldn't put her in a nursing home, but eventually he hired a live-in caregiver when he could no longer manage on his own. I wondered how he remained calm and upbeat as his partner of more than fifty years faded.

At a family gathering last summer, I watched her caregiver patiently hold a spoon to Ruthie's mouth, encouraging her to eat, waiting for the swallow reflex to kick in. She told me she worked with Ruthie every day, helping her to use a walker, to take a few halting steps. At eighty-two, Ruthie was more or less healthy physically, but Hal told me that a brain scan revealed big empty spaces inside her skull. When she can no longer swallow, my mom said they will not insert a feeding tube. Will my beloved aunt—baker of angel food cake, pecan loaf, carrot ring, and other treats—eventually starve to death?

It's hard to call anyone with Alzheimer's lucky. But at least Ruthie is not prone to the paranoia and belligerence that plague many with the disease. Ruthie's doctor told her family that she has a "happy" dementia, something that, apparently, is not so uncommon. I read a story in *Newsweek* recently where the writer likened her mother's "pleasant dementia" to the state of serenity one seeks from meditation. Maybe all those years of TM paid off.

*

On a recent visit to Ruthie and Hal's, my extended family gathered over take-out Chinese food. It hit me that there would be no more of my aunts' home-cooked meals, ever. The breath of time and pulse of decline, rampaging through the generation ahead of me, were prickling up my scalp, urging me to take heed. After dinner, I asked Uncle Hal if he still had Ruthie's braids. "Somewhere, yes," he said. "I'm sure we still have them."

Even now, I can feel their weight in my hands.

CAL IN GAUZE II
Jeff Blank
photograph
9x6

IN YOUR NORTH SEA DREAM

Jeff Alfier

Leave your flat, deep in the city,
take the longest loop around the harbor, study
the day's early shipping: hulks making for docks,
inbound from the Aberdeen—Lerwick run,
the clang of freight and foghorn, shouts of dock
men, shunted cargo, the groan of diesel.

Turn back down Guild to the rail
station and forget for a moment what the harbor
may mean, how it treads your mind like the past,
as you search destinations that would carry you
on some undulant, overland pace far out of the city.

Reach the open area of grass
along River Dee, where your father drifted
in drunken sleep after endless days at the quarry.
The spot is vacant now, trimmed green and perfect.

Consider the day's final departures—
downcountry to Dundee, or inland to some nether
loch. How once urgent tickets, punched and castoff,
fly in gusting drafts of wind, a sound now louder
than your steps retracing the sea.

GHOSTS

Jack Carenza

In 1882 god died; excuse me,
God died; the same year the first
radical mastectomy was successfully
performed, removing both breasts
and the death sentence from breast cancer.
That year Ibsen's *Ghosts* premiered
in Chicago, drawing an audience's tears.
Ghosts of tears, of god, of men with
breastless wives, of mutilated malignant
breasts ping ponged between the chests of
Nietzsche and my great grandmother Ida;
the only two in Aura Turner Hall that night.
Darwin (who died that year) lodged himself in Ida's
right breast and Dr. William Stewart Halsted
scooped out the poisoned pectoralis, axilla
and lymph nodes, like the overripe flesh
of a cantaloupe. Just west of Turner Hall
the Cincinnati Red Stockings and my Chicago
White Sox played in the first ever World Series.
Nietzsche supported the German-led Reds,
Darwin supported the fittest, and God

was buried in a White Sox shirt alongside
my mother, the number ten fending eyes
from the sizeable lacuna of a left breast.
Darwin and Nietzsche and Halsted and Ida
and Ibsen and God and   are dead,
but they left *The sun.— The sun.**

*From Ibsen's *Ghosts,* 1882.

FIVE POEMS

Michael St. Germain

silhouette
of leafless tree
stunning in
fine tracery

pretty shell
dead inside
lacquered by
retreating tide

line of sun
dot of rain
simple
existential plane

corridors
of thought sublime
dimly lit
and full of grime

harmony
in soot and lead
pigeon soaring
overhead

REACH
Tyler Quintin
charcoal
19x25

THE CAT STORY

Richard K. Weems

An old woman shows up at my door to tell me my cat is dead. This after I've spent all morning and a good part of the afternoon getting ready to hang myself. The old woman is at least seventy, nearly toothless, disheveled. She carries a paper sack, the bottom rounded at the edges like a curling puck.

"It was a Buick who did it," she says. She thumbs over her shoulder toward the street, where there is no Buick. No aura of recent death, no hint of an accident. I don't know why I'm even looking. I don't have a cat. My gaze strays to the neighbors' lawns—manicured, sculpted, uniform. The kind of neighborhood that will shudder with disgust at a local hanging.

"A Buick?" I say. "How do you know it's my cat?"

"Your cat," she says. She scratches her scalp through her shower cap. "Got hit in front of your house."

If she has the cat in that sack, it's balled up pretty tight. The mouth of the sack is worn in her grip.

"Who sent you?" I haven't ventured to open the door wider than the width of my face. This isn't even my house—it's my grandmother Peg's—but she's in Florida for the season and I'm supposed to be getting my life back together. Obviously, Peg's offer hasn't done much good.

"I got nothing to do with nothing," the old woman says. "Thought I was doing a favor. You can just bury it out back you know." Artfully, she looks around and above me, avoiding my eyes with precise near-misses.

How long has she walked around with that cat? She must have walked for days from the looks of her. Her quilted housecoat has grass and mud stains that make its true color hard to discern. "What if I told you I didn't have a cat?"

"Liar," she says, still scratching her head.

"Maybe it's best you came in." I'm already quite an item of gossip in this neighborhood, the equivalent of an idiot-manchild locked away in the root cellar. Now, Peg's poor excuse of a grandson, who's given up stability and marriage for artistic endeavor, is making things worse by humoring a dirty homeless woman on the front stoop. I can feel the neighbors watching us, their property values sinking into their lower intestines. I open the door all the way.

Her slippered feet slap against the tile floor. She keeps a gentle hand under the bottom of the sack, reinforcing it but reverential about not poking its contents.

I hesitate from offering her a seat. There's the kitchen chair I brought out so I could do my business with the light fixture, but it's in exactly the right spot and I don't want to go through all that rigmarole again. This being my grandmother Peg's house, the sofa, loveseat and armchair are all covered in plastic, but still I worry that the old woman's grime will seep through. Bad enough I plan to leave behind a swinging body to clean up, but also the stink of a filthy old lunatic and her dead cat? I motion toward the kitchen chair. "Sit?"

The old woman sits with determination and plops the sack onto her lap. More of a thud. The sack has some serious weight to it.

I take my seat on the sofa, directly across from her so there we are, face to face, the coffee table and my rejected book between us like a wall built far too low. I reach for my glass of gin but think better of it. I have no intention of offering her any. The generic rejection letter clipped to my book reads, "Dear Writer." I haven't read the rest; with an opening like that, why bother? I doodled next to their salutation so it now reads, "Dear Writer-my-ass."

The old woman sits up as though ready to withstand police interrogation. She has every intention of protecting the sack in her lap.

"Coke?" she says abruptly. "Coke? You got Coke here?"

"It's all warm," I lie. "It's sitting in a cupboard."

"A little ice will do the trick. I can help you dig that hole if you give me a Coke."

I sink deeply into the sofa, the kind of sofa that's a struggle to get up from again. To the right of my book sits my phone. Three new messages—all from my wife, one every other day for the past week, each one no doubt prompted by grandmother Peg, a new effort to pull me out of my hole. I watched each one pop up on my home screen after the electronic bloop. The first one said, *Hello Brad, it's Marsha.* Then, *Hope you're doing better. Been thinking of you.* The most recent, *Call me if you want.* Grandmother Peg no doubt floated some promise of inheritance if Marsha took me back. I haven't found any reason to respond.

*

I'm not the type anyone would have ever taken for a writer, including me—a stable though generally unaffectionate marriage, a well-off and aging grandmother, and a steady job as Associate Manager of Space for a 40-story office building, my prime responsibility chair inventory and allocation. I was going over inventory sheets in my office one day, and I suddenly wanted to have Charlie Rose interview me about my novel. I thought what an interesting story my sudden, unprompted calling would make to start off the interview.

I brought home a dozen legal pads that night and stacked them on the piano in the den. All through dinner, as Marsha fished for compliments on her brown rice with wakami, I wrote questions Charlie Rose might ask me so I would have some natural-sounding, thoughtful responses: *How do you know you weren't just struck by a sudden bout of midlife crisis?* and *Talk about how the position of Associate Manager of Space prepared you to be such a methodical and assertive novelist.* After dinner I went straight to the den and made a start. The going was tough, since I had to make things up from scratch. After she finished loading the dishes, Marsha came into the den with an exotic food catalog. She sat on the edge of the recliner as though in a doctor's waiting room and opened the catalog, but she didn't read a thing.

"How long does a novel take?" she asked, her pretty brown eyes trying their best to understand something about what I was doing.

"I write for a while," I said, stooped over the cover of the piano keys, "and then it will be finished." I didn't have much yet—a description of some weather, and a guy coming home from work. Marsha said, "Hmm," as though she understood perfectly, and went back to her catalog. The turning of pages sounded like jelly slapped through a ventilation grate.

"It can't be all that long," she said. Marsha didn't read novels. Magazines were practical and functional, catalogs an utter necessity, though she would sometimes admire the layout of the cover on a Clive Cussler or a John Grisham I was reading. "I mean, if it took all that long, it wouldn't be worth all that bother, would it?" As she spoke, I could feel my brain numbing, acupuncture on the hypothalamus.

"You need to leave me alone," I said. Marsha looked at me as if I had just told her she had a cancerous bulb on her cheek. "You need to get out and leave me alone," I said. Funny—not once had I asked Charlie Rose to give me a moment to thank my patient and understanding wife.

Marsha closed the catalog and held it to her chest as she left.

As I wrote, it was all think and drink, think and drink, write a little, then back to the thinking and the drinking. I went right to it every day after work, all morning and afternoon on my days off. In the evenings I slept off the heavy drunk I accumulated during the day. Marsha checked up on me every now and then. I could smell hope, like moldy water, swell up in her when she'd find me slumped uncomfortably in the leather recliner or reading the label on a bottle of Wild Turkey, my messy pages scattered around the piano.

"I'm making dinner," she'd say for instance, her voice tinged with a hint of warning, of her need for things to be normal again. "Do you want me to put lemon in the curry?" Maybe she counted on me to announce failure so she could comfort me briefly and pack me an alfalfa salad for lunch the next day, our life back to brief kisses and semi-annual intimacy. I ignored her the best I could, feeling with her every intrusion a desire to throw pencils at her ankles.

So I wrote at the office, chair requests and locations ignored or handled sloppily to let me focus on my real work. The office building fell into chaos, unclaimed task chairs stranded in hallways, mail sorters sorting in leather executive high-backs. Marsha hid my manuscript pages, so I put her silk blouses in the dryer on high. She said, "Oh, great," every time she saw me with a pen. I slept in the living room and promised things would be back to normal when I finished. It took three months of note pads and pens and pencils and bottles of liquor that fueled my creative fire, and getting fired to boot, but I finished my novel. I told Marsha our troubles would be over when I typed it up and got it published. She did her best to pretend I didn't live in the house anymore while I researched agents and book publishers. As I sent my novel out, I imagined the letter of acceptance, rife with compliments. I planned my book tour, practiced my mannerisms, invented witticisms to sign my name under. Late at night, I could hear Marsha crying on the phone. I imagined literate groupies, bodies tingling in my presence. With each rejection, I moved my book from one envelope to the next, sure that this time someone would see the light.

My grandmother Peg lent me her house when Marsha finally asked me to leave. Marsha never asked me directly, to tell the truth. She told grandmother Peg, and grandmother Peg told me. Marsha wouldn't make any effort to talk to me except to pull open the zippers on my best pants. In retaliation, I sawed into the straps of her bras with a nail file so they would break while she was wearing them.

Grandmother Peg's offer was not one of kindness. It was to get this 'writing thing' out of me, to let it run its course like a stomach virus. She sent me the keys express mail. That night, she called from her larger house in Florida.

"The summer house is yours," she said. "Send your book to every name you can find. See how no one wants it and for God's sake go back to Marsha.

"And also for God's sake, Brad," she added. She paused to let her next statement sink in. "Brad. Brad. Dry out and give up and go back to your life." This was four months ago, and she told me she was going to need the house again in four and a half.

None of this sounds like good justification for a hanging, but I've given up on finding a good reason. I spent most of the morning making sure the chair was in the right place so I could stand on it comfortably with the belt around my neck and kick the chair away easily to give me no way of backing out. Then I started doing dry runs, swinging by my arms to make sure the light fixture would hold me up long enough to kill me, each run separated by an hour on the couch, where I drank and got my courage up for another go. It's one thing to practice your death, another to get off the couch to practice it again. Just before the old woman came knocking, I was wondering if I was up for a dress rehearsal.

*

"About this cat," I say to the old woman.

"Your cat," she says defensively, "out in the road nothing I could do about that. Just sitting there doing what cats do in the middle of the road acting like nothing's going to happen to him safe as all shit and suddenly there's this car this Mazda this brown shoebox thing."

"A Buick?" I say.

"Yes a Buick I said Buick no way you can prove otherwise." The woman scootches up a little, her housecoat crackling. "This here Buick isn't from around here it was obvious speeding down the road in a neighborhood like this a nice neighborhood like this one speeding down the road like that the cat had it coming. You can bury it under a tree in some shade."

I'm ready for her to pull the cat out of her sack by the hind legs and lay it out on the coffee table like a butcher displaying a plucked chicken. I move my rejected book aside. I notice how much "Writer-my-ass" stands out, along with my doodles around the clean, mock-literary typeface of the company letterhead. The font that suggests serenity and insight. The doodles are of hanged stick figures. I can't remember how many times my book has been rejected now, but it seems to come back more quickly every time I send it out. I slide the rejection note from under the paper clip and gradually turn it over.

Meanwhile, the old woman is still at it: "And if you think I blame that Buick that Chevy any you think wrong. But boy was it coming down the road coming down quick cuz he couldn't have known what kind of neighborhood it was not being from around here and Friskie got it all in one shot at least just got run over and shut his eyes and that was that."

"Friskie?" I pet the rejection slip until it's flat.

"You named him," she says. She points to make sure I know who thought up that stupid name. "All those cats how are you going to find an original name for all of them? He likes Friskies so you call him Friskie. The black and white you call Oreo what else? Sylvester the other black and white. Mittens Cracker Big Balls you can't go not giving them names you know." She looks sentimental and a little misty-eyed talking about my cats.

"How many cats in all?"

She slumps as though strategic wires have been cut. A look of futility. "Your damn cat mister," she says.

*

The sun is coming down. The shades at the old woman's back glow appropriately. I have one hand on my rejected book; I am considering whether to leave it behind or destroy it before I go.

The book I've written is this:

A business prospector, Phil, depressed and stuck in his job, quits and runs off to Mexico, where he beds Latina identical twins and tries his hand at bounty hunting after a chance meeting with a one-eyed midget who gives him cryptic advice about life over a session of tequila. Phil finds he has a knack for this kind of work, and on his first time out he brings to justice the head of a notorious drug cartel and steals a briefcase full of drug money that befriended

DEA agents discover but let him drive off with in a scene of touching camaraderie. Phil returns home, determined to resume his life now that he's sown his wild oats. But the suburban lifestyle leaves him wanting, and after a well honed and witty speech to his patient but unsympathetic wife, something like the end of *A Doll's House* with muscle, he goes off into the night, his future uncertain but chock-full of potential for gunplay.

The old woman suddenly pulls a faded pea green scarf from the pocket of her housecoat.

"I make these myself," she says, the silk scarf crumpled in her hand, a far cry from any kind of lucrative presentation. "You got four dollars? I could use four dollars right now. Four dollars and a ride."

It's not what she says or how she says it, but something about the old woman inspires the perfect idea in me.

"I write," I tell her.

She glances sidelong at me, the first time our eyes have met. She rubs her cheek with the scarf, and she clutches the paper sack a little tighter, as though I've just told her I'm a rapist of old women. "You make money with that?"

"I just write," I tell her.

"Not buying no damn story," she says. "And I'm not taking one for this scarf. Don't need that shit. Don't need to be carrying around no story I got nothing to do with," she says.

"But you do," I tell her.

Again, the brief meeting of the eyes. If we go on like this, we'll be married by nightfall.

"You drunk?" she says. "All I need is a dollar."

"It's a story about cats," I tell her. "Cats and scarves and grandmothers who wrap everything they own in plastic. It's got all the reasons why you can't go home anymore. It's about being down to dill pickles in the fridge, about the last days of the siege.

Coke with no ice and the wives who leave their men because their men like Coke that way. It's about the clarity that happens sometimes right before the end." All this comes together in me like particles orbiting a gravity well, collapsing into the inevitable brilliance of a new star.

"That's a weird story," she says.

"I'll send you a copy."

"Don't read no damn stories." She lifts the sack to her chest and stands. "Don't got no goddamn stories cuz I don't need no goddamn stories and they got nothing to do with me I ain't in no goddamn goddamn story." She makes for the door. "Fucking stories no ice this house smells like pork like a fucking pig." Before she leaves, she pauses a moment in the doorway. "Great stinking pig is how it smells I won't give my tits to know how you keep your pecker up in here!"

I sit up. The couch creaks like couches in a grandmother's house do. I hear the old woman still yelling out about my pecker and all as she rumbles down the street.

It's a beautiful ending—the perfect idea that doesn't get written, its only living vestiges rolling in pieces around the head of an old woman trying to find her kitty's final resting place. I rise and take my novel out back to toss it. I'll leave nothing behind but a half bottle of gin, some Cuervo and a little apricot brandy. Let them admire nothing but the strength of the knot in my belt, how I chose the stem of the light fixture rather than the paltry branches to swing from. An artist's death. Grandmother Peg will shudder in disappointment at the thought of me. Marsha won't be able to contain her anger. I am past needing affirmation for my work. I feel more ready now than I have all day.

Out back, I pause over the trashcan. I consider digging a hole in the yard, but some birds nearby distract me. They're small, brown birds, I don't know what kind. Quick and electric in movement, but deceptively preoccupied. They seem too easy and inviting to reach out, grab and crush. My manuscript lands with a loud slap on top of yesterday's trash, and I go back inside.

MOSS AND FROG
Abby Miller
watercolor
9x12

MONUMENT

Andrew Jarvis

The wood of the wheelbarrow, too dead
to deliver any bushel of brush,
is orgasmic, enlivened by lichen.

She pushed it here, exhausted her muscle
to build fires in days burning to nights;
a monument to her work, it blazes

a lush embellishment of evergreen
bodies, as if colonized by cosmic
orbs of gas, atmospheric and blooming.

White and green seep into yellow, then black
bursts along the wooden plane, where her hands
held onto color, the crimson handles

of years decomposing in parasites,
symbiotic, breathing, biologic;
in her afterlife, they grip, then thrive.

TYING FLIES

B.J. Best

it's the wisp
of a wink,
the featherweight
of a moment,
the tiny argument
of a thread
with its knots.
in the tackle box
lives the recipe
for a fish fry, yes;
but also a prayer
that curses the god
who made sunken logs,
seaweed, and rocks.

LA DERNIÈRE FEUILLE

Théophile Gautier

Dans la forêt chauve et rouillée
Il ne reste plus au rameau
Qu'une pauvre feuille oubliée,
Rien qu'une feuille et qu'un oiseau,

Il ne reste plus dans mon âme
Qu'un seul amour pour y chanter;
Mais le vent d'automne qui brame
Ne permet pas de l'écouter.

L'oiseau s'en va, la feuille tombe,
L'amour s'éteint, car c'est l'hiver.
Petit oiseau, viens sur ma tombe
Chanter, quand l'arbre sera vert.

THÉOPHILE GAUTIER: THE LAST LEAF

Translated by Len Krisak

In the forest, rusted bare,
The branches' leaves are all but gone.
One drab, forgotten leaf hangs there.
A single leaf. A bird alone.

There's nothing left inside my soul
But one last love that lives to sing,
Though autumn gales that rage and howl
Allow no ear the listening.

One flies, one falls, that none can save.
Love dies when it is winter then.
Come, meager bird. Come to my grave
To sing, when woods are green again.

CONDEMNED PROPERTY

John C. Mannone

After the woodborer beetle killed the pine trees
in the backyard, the lumbermen felled them.
Left remnants entwined with
barbed wire that used to fence the fields. The bugs
moved out to plague another grove of trees.
Now, new growth jungles the property.
Redbud and maple sprouts seem to make weeds
look prettier than they are, they hide
a garage, too, paint peeling on dryrot-wood.
The pit inside, once doubled-up for mechanic-ing cars
and for the sheltering from tornadoes, is now full
of old rainwash and debris that's fallen-in
shaken from shelves by an unforgiving night wind
and maybe by my old worthless cat stalking mice
she fails to catch.
But the old ceramic-lined satellite dish—once white,
but now stained moss green—is still poised
as if shouting its mildew voice to heaven
while a black walnut tree waves its branches
over the horn of its mouth
as if to hush it, to keep it from speaking
about everything it saw and heard in the rundown house
when a man and his wife lived there
before their yelling at each other withered
the vines, and the grasses that were once green too.
Now, only ghosts remain, too tired to complain
on who's going to mow the lawn—
even I don't listen to them anymore,
and I still live there.

MILES DAVIS
Huascar Medina
mixed media
24x30

THE BLUE HOUSE

Greg Jenkins

The clock on the dash reads exactly 11:00 a.m. as Mike and Grace Twigg pull up to the blue house just outside Zurich. The appointed hour. He parks the black BMW, hauls his massive frame out of the car and goes around to assist his wife. Both are dressed neatly but casually—he in a polo shirt and jeans, she in a blouse and cropped pants—and they might be taken for a typical middle-aged American couple on vacation.

But they aren't on vacation.

Nor is the midnight blue house a place where anyone lives as such. People work there and people die there, but it's nothing like a home. A two-story box, rather severe in its plainness, it's surrounded by trees and shrubs and abutted by a pond that's filled with flashing goldfish. The Twiggs will use a planked, wooden walkway to cross the pond and reach the house's entrance. Today is a "good day" for Grace, so with the aid of a cane and some support from her husband, she's able to hobble along at a reasonable pace.

Grasping her elbow, Mike glances up at the sky, which is clear and cerulean. Postcard perfect.

*

Thirty years before, they first met on a spring day every bit as clement as this one. Mike was walking through a parking lot at Indiana State University, having just finished a chem class. He was a grad student there, as was Grace. Not far from his own vehicle, which in those days was something less than a BMW, a young man was yelling aggressively, face-to-face, at a young woman.

Though the young man was by far the louder and more active of the two, it was the young woman—Grace—who drew most of Mike's attention. Petite and winsome, with curly brown hair that jounced when she bobbed her head to make a point of her own, she absolutely refused to take a backward step. From very close range, her adversary, a soon-to-be ex-boyfriend it would turn out, leaned down and shook his fist at her.

"You better damn well *think* about what you're doing," he said.

An old-fashioned type who still believed in chivalry, Mike went over and stepped between the two.

"No," he said, poking the young man's chest with a thick finger, "you better think about what *you're* doing."

Abruptly staring up at his opponent rather than down, his poles reversed, the young man seemed to find a grudging wisdom in Mike's words. Within a few seconds he was slinking away, muttering to himself.

That evening Mike took Grace out for a drink, and she told him in that frank way of hers that she could've handled the twerp just fine by herself. Mike said nothing, though his eyes approved of her spunk.

"Still," she said, "I appreciate your help. It was very good of you."

Smiling, he held up his green bottle of Rolling Rock and offered her a toast.

"To a beautiful and brave lady," he said.

It was the start of a happy union that would not only last but prosper for decades. And while neither had a taste for alcohol especially, from that first night on, if the occasion was special enough, they'd mark it by sharing a drink or two.

*

This isn't the Twiggs' first visit to the blue house (though it does figure to be their last). So they have a certain familiarity with the grounds, with the house itself and with some of the people inside. At the door they are greeted warmly by Dr. Katarina Engel, whom they address simply as "Katarina." As always, she's wearing horn-rimmed glasses and an immaculate white lab coat. With her cheery blue eyes and gentle manner, she might've done well, one suspects, as a childcare worker or a kindergarten instructor. Escorting the visitors inside the house, she banters easily with them.

"Did you sleep last night?" Katarina asks, her German accent barely detectable.

Mike shrugs.

Grace answers: "Oh, yes."

"And did you have some breakfast this morning?"

Mike nods.

"At Maison Blunt," Grace says.

"Ah," says Katarina. "Of course. Not far from the Hauptbahnhof."

"I enjoyed the Moroccan theme," Grace puts in. "And the garden out back is marvelous, don't you think?"

Katarina agrees and leads them to the kitchen—or what would ordinarily be considered the kitchen. She has them sit at a table. Apologizing for the bureaucratic nature of things, she presents them with two pens and a final sheaf of documents.

"It will take only a moment," she promises. "I know it's an imposition, but in these cases our government is—ah—very particular."

"Perfectly understandable," Grace assures her.

Quietly the Twiggs provide signatures, initials and dates where required. As the central player, Grace must use her pen more often than her husband, and, because of her condition, her hand moves more slowly and laboriously.

*

The paperwork finished, Katarina revisits the forthcoming procedure, even though she's already discussed it with them several times. As the doctor speaks, Grace tilts into her words, listening it seems not just with her ears but with her entire being. Mike listens too, but his hulking body speaks a different language. Slouched in his chair, he moves his eyes restlessly from the floor to the ceiling to the Swiss railway clock on the wall, its red second hand pausing briefly at the top of each new minute.

"I will serve as a witness," Katarina says. "Gretchen here will be our second witness."

A flick of her eyes causes Mike to turn and see a young woman, tall and slim, her face expressionless, standing behind him. Until now, he'd been unaware of her hovering presence. She's holding a small black camcorder, the device already operating.

"Everything," Katarina says, "will be digitally recorded as well."

Yesterday they had a dress rehearsal. Grace drank down without stopping a small glass of water, maybe six ounces, to prove that she could. Half an hour later she did so again. (Katarina warned that an inability to chug successfully would cause problems.) Today Grace will again drink twice: first a drug to prevent vomiting, and then later a powerful barbiturate—a "poison," as the doctor unambiguously calls it. The poison will result in a relatively quick and serviceable death.

"Now," Katarina says, looking solely at Grace, "it's up to you when we begin. Or even *if* we begin." Her voice is soft as ever, but also clipped and precise.

Grace glances at Mike, a pro forma glance, not really seeking anything more than a moment's contact, and then brings her gaze to bear on Katarina.

"I can see no point in delaying," Grace says.

"You're sure?"

"I'm sure."

With that, Katarina rises and goes to a different table, a smaller one, on which various bottles, vials, glasses, napkins and the like have been carefully arranged. She opens a bottle and pours a murky orangish liquid into a glass. She then brings the glass over to Grace and holds it out to her.

"This is the antiemetic," Katarina says. "Do you wish to drink it?"

"I do."

"You're sure?"

"I am."

As rehearsed, Grace accepts the glass, brings it to her lips and downs the liquid without hesitation. A steady succession of controlled and deliberate swallows. Next to her, Mike sets his square jaw tightly, clears his throat but says nothing. His rugged face, so like the face of a Marine colonel or a retired football player, is already beginning to blanch.

*

Within the past two years Grace began having physical problems—dropping things, stumbling, generally feeling that something peculiar and insidious was happening to her. She went to a series of specialists, two of whom, then three, finally diagnosed her with motor neuron disease. An unusually fast-moving form of it. At the time, she was fifty-one years old. Already she has difficulty standing and walking, sometimes her hands and arms twitch, and she must concentrate on enunciating her words; occasionally she slurs them.

"What can be done about this?" she'd asked.

Nothing, the doctors told her, though it took them a great many words to shape the message. No, the condition would advance continuously until in the end she'd be totally helpless. Death would occur by suffocation.

"Well, I can't have this," she told her husband. "I won't have it."

"So what will you do?" Mike asked her. "You can't just . . . I mean, you can't simply . . ."

"Kill myself?"

He nodded.

"No, you're right," she said, and he relaxed somewhat. "I wouldn't know how," she said. "Someone who knows about these things will have to help us."

Mike didn't care for the idea of assisted death, and he told her so directly and repeatedly. It went against his principles. Then again, he didn't care for the idea of her being gravely ill either; that also went against his principles. His wife being as determined as she was, he guessed she would ultimately get her way, and maybe that would be to the good. Or maybe not. Who the hell could genuinely know? He felt confused, and in his own way he was (and still is) almost as stricken as Grace.

Yet he felt no doubt whatever about Grace's steely resolve. Her ability to make up her mind about a course of action and then stick to it was legendary, as Mike or anyone else who knew her could attest. Still in her thirties, she quit her job as a grade school teacher when she saw an opportunity to take over a local trucking company. Mike, who'd parlayed his chemistry degree into a respectable career in the perfume industry, was immediately skeptical. Why give up a reliable income to take such a risk? Besides, it was strange enough that he was in perfume; now his wife wanted to run a trucking firm? Something in this picture felt out of whack to him and his old-school values.

"What do you know about trucks?" he asked her.

"Not much," she admitted. "So I'll have to learn."

Which she certainly did. Working fanatically, she built her company in the span of a few years into a multi-million dollar enterprise.

Then, over his protests, she turned around and sold it.

"Good God," he said. "Why? It's doing great."

Because, Grace explained, the trucking project had merely been a means to an end—financial independence. Now, she said, they'd have the time and resources to do whatever they wanted. To travel abroad, for instance.

Mike, who despite his smarts was stubbornly provincial, didn't necessarily *want* to travel; staying at home suited him well enough. "I'll take the USA anytime," he said. But she kept after him. "Just open your mind a little," she suggested. When at last he gave in and spent a week with her on the French Riviera, he suddenly adopted a whole new outlook. "Say," he said, lounging on the golden beach in Cannes, "this is pretty sweet."

*

As everyone in the blue house knows, it will take thirty minutes or so for the first drug, the one that prepares the stomach for the poison, to take effect. In the meantime there's little to do but wait. For the most part Mike sits silently beside Grace; now and then he gets up to take a short stroll—to gaze at the potted plants or at the pastoral paintings that hang on the white walls. He would talk to his wife, but it seems to him that all the words—thousands and thousands of them—have been used up. Everything has been said; everything decided. Now it's simply a matter of staying the course.

So he allows his mind to drift away to some of the wonderful and exotic places they've visited over the years. Paris. Rome. Barcelona. He remembers the time they walked the Ramblas, the main boulevard in the Old City of Barcelona. Starting at the Plaça de Catalunya, they went all the way to the waterfront, passing en route an old opera house, elegant cafes, fragrant flower stands and even an outdoor bird market. Quite a walk, and at the end of it, Mike and not Grace was a tad weary. After enjoying some tapas, they commemorated the day by sipping a glass of Tío Pepe.

Then there was the trip to Ireland, which they took just before the onset of her illness. One evening they'd concluded a delicious dinner in a Galway pub when, without warning, a band began to play a selection of Irish traditional music. Fiddle, flute, banjo, pipes. The music was loud and throbbed with energy, and at some point people got up and started doing a stylized folk dance. On impulse, the Twiggs decided to join them. Capering around with only the vaguest notion of what to do and when, they hoped that their sheer gusto might compensate for their obvious lack of skill.

Perhaps it did.

When eventually they returned to their table, a redheaded man approached them and said something to them in a joshing, lighthearted way. Mike couldn't understand him since he'd spoken in Irish, not English. To Mike's astonishment, Grace, laughing, replied to the man in his own language. The man chuckled and went on his way.

"How . . ." Mike stammered. "How the devil . . ."

"I did some research," she said, "back home. Common words and phrases. I wanted to be prepared."

Mike shook his head and ordered a pint of Guinness for her and another for him. They drank the "black stuff" in celebration of a memorable day.

*

Standing near his wife in the blue house, he is overtaken by a keen urge to speak to her—to say *some*thing, however trivial or banal.

"Grace," he ventures with some awkwardness, "hasn't the weather been fine lately?"

Blinking, she turns to peer up at him. Unlike his, her face seems relaxed and even serene. "Yes," she says. "Very pretty."

"Weather like this, you know, it takes me back to other times. Other places."

In response, she inclines her head slightly.

"Yesterday," he goes on, "when we were looking out at Lake Zurich, it looked so—I don't know—so perfect. There was the pale blue of the sky, and then the deeper blue of the water. . . . For the life of me I couldn't tell which blue I liked better. They were both so . . ."

"Yes."

"It's a nice color, either way," he says.

"It is," she agrees. She is smiling faintly, and he is smiling too.

He would summon something further to say, something richer and more meaningful, but the words elude him. He has the sense that he's caught in an oppressive dream, and he wants—needs—to awaken. But he can't.

Without a sound, and at a discreet distance, Gretchen has floated almost wraithlike into view, the black camcorder running. Seconds later, the horn-rimmed glasses and white lab coat follow her into the room. Automatically Katarina commands the Twiggs' attention.

"It's been about thirty minutes," she says softly. Her eyes meet with Grace's. "I assume you've decided?"

"I decided a long time ago," Grace says.

"Do you wish to proceed?"

"Yes."

"You will drink the poison?"

"I have no choice."

At this, Katarina frowns and raises her right hand, slender fingers spread wide apart. "You do have a choice," she says firmly. "You do have a choice."

"Well then," Grace says, "I choose to move ahead. I choose to drink the poison."

*

As scripted, Mike, his face pallid, helps his wife to her feet, and they move to a puffy white sofa in the next room where she'll be more comfortable. The sofa will also be better able to accommodate her collapse than will a kitchen chair. Meanwhile Katarina lingers behind in the kitchen mixing the lethal drink. Gretchen has positioned herself between the two rooms, slowly pivoting her electronic eye in one direction and then the other.

When Katarina emerges, she is carrying a glass of water. In the water a white powdery substance, the pentobarbital, dances like a tiny snowstorm.

She stands before Grace, glass uplifted.

"This is the poison," Katarina says. "Do you wish to drink it?"

"Yes," Grace answers.

"Drinking the poison will cause you to die," Katarina says. "So let me ask you again: Are you *certain* you wish to drink it?"

"Quite certain." Without further comment from anyone, Katarina hands the glass to Grace. Much as she did thirty minutes before, she lifts it to her lips and consumes the contents in a strong series of gulps. The act takes just a few seconds. Politely, she hands the glass back to Katarina.

Seated at Grace's side, Mike has been caught off-guard by the suddenness of her last act. He understood it would happen, but why so fast? Not that it would've changed anything had she been more deliberate. But he thought perhaps she might've made a statement first, a brief summing up or a valediction, or that Katarina would've conducted some sort of preliminary ceremony. Something! But poor Grace just swilled down that awful stuff so quickly. As if in a rush. And now—

Now will come sleep, then a coma, then death.

He watches her carefully. No change yet. Oddly, he feels in this terrible moment he must do what he can to aid her, to shield her from harm as he did long ago during their first encounter in that faraway parking lot. But this is precisely what he's forbidden from doing.

When Grace finally breaks her silence, it's as if she's been reading his thoughts. "It's no one's fault," she says. "Certainly not yours, Mike. It's just how it is." She kisses his cheek and tells him goodbye. "Be strong," she says.

Unable to speak, he holds her in his arms.

"You know," she adds, as if from a vast distance, "I believed in Santa Claus till I was nine years old ..."

In a minute her head slumps, and she's asleep, breathing lightly. Then heavily. In another minute the breathing softens again and then gradually fades away. Ceases. So smooth was the transition that Mike, still holding her, couldn't have pinpointed the exact instant she died.

*

For a long while he continues to sit there, his brawny arms around her, his face virtually the same color as the sofa, the walls, the laundered lab coat. Katarina nods at Gretchen, and the little light on the camcorder winks out, and Gretchen withdraws to another part of the blue house.

At length Mike gently releases his wife. He tries to stand but doesn't quite make it. On his second attempt he succeeds, albeit shakily.

"I'll certify her death," Katarina tells him. "We'll have some people come by to take care of the body."

"This was her choice," he says numbly.

"Of course."

"It was the *right* choice," he says, as if testing the assertion's merit.

"She felt it was."

Mike runs his hand over his stubbly jaw but otherwise doesn't move.

"Is there anything I can get you?" Katarina asks.

"I'm all right."

"Would you care for a drink?"

Given the circumstances, the innocent question sends a weird shock, a frisson, rocketing through him.

"A drink!" he says. He stares down at her.

"A glass of juice," she clarifies. "A cup of tea. I can get you a shot of whiskey if you like."

He collects himself. Glancing back at his wife, he runs his hand over his jaw once more. "A drink," he repeats.

"If you like."

He requests a shot of whiskey.

"What kind?" she asks.

"Doesn't matter."

She goes away and returns with a shot glass and a bottle of bonded bourbon. Mike pours himself a full shot and turns to Grace, who's reclining on the sofa, hands on her lap, eyes closed. A tableau.

He raises his glass, holds it toward her.

"To a beautiful and brave lady," he says, and drinks the shot in one quick swallow.

SONG AND DANCE
Barbara Waterman-Peters
oil on canvas
18x24

LOVESICK APPEAL

Brett Foster

I beg you, nimble Mercury,
climb down from that fountain.
The time's come to usher
my ghostly heart back toward the pain

of life above, amid a world
that cares less than nothing
when loss's flag's unfurled.
Bring me to meadows, at evening.

Will I ever be blessed again
to see Bettina cross
Folly Bridge in the rain,
seen from the warm pub's enclosure?

Please just allow her to return
a while, asleep in love's trance,
pleasure-tired, unconcerned
about her morning elegance.

CONTRIBUTORS

Jeff Alfier won the 2014 Kithara Book Prize for his poetry collection *Idyll for a Vanishing River* (Glass Lyre Press, 2013). He is also author of *The Wolf Yearling* (Silver Birch Press, 2013) and *The Storm Petrel—Ireland Poems* (Grayson Books, 2014).

B.J. Best is the author of three books of poetry: *But Our Princess Is in Another Castle* (Rose Metal Press, 2013), *Birds of Wisconsin* (New Rivers Press, 2010), and *State Sonnets* (sunnyoutside, 2009). *I got off the train at Ash Lake*, a verse novella, is forthcoming from sunnyoutside. He lives in Wisconsin.

Jeff Blank is a Kansas City fine-art photographer (among other things). He has been shooting for more than 30 years and specializes in long exposures, Blank and White and film photography. His recent "Glassworks" series incorporates rusted metal manipulation with his photography to further explore textural elements in his artwork.

Jack Carenza is a 24-year-old poet from The Rose of New England (Norwich, Connecticut). Aside from his poetic pursuits, he is an avid outdoorsman, an independent hip-hop artist, and corn chowder connoisseur.

Susana H. Case's newest book is *4 Rms w Vu* (Mayapple Press, 2014). Author of four full-length poetry collections and four chapbooks, including *The Scottish Café*, which was re-released in a Polish-English version, *Kawiarnia Szkocka*, by Opole

University Press, she is a professor at the New York Institute of Technology.

Shannon Draper teaches English at Lawrence High School in Lawrence, Kansas, and holds an M.A. in English from Kansas State University. Her work has appeared in *Artwhore, Touchstone Literary Journal, Blood Lotus* and *The Midwest Quarterly.* She writes best in a quiet room with an open window.

Brett Foster, who died at age 42 in November 2015, was the author of two full-length poetry collections, *The Garbage Eater* and the forthcoming *Extravagant Rescues*, both from Northwestern University Press. A professor of English at Wheaton College and a former Stegner Fellow at Stanford University, he published work in *Boston Review, Hudson Review, IMAGE, Kenyon Review, Poetry Daily, Raritan, Southwest Review* and *Yale Review.*

Théophile Gautier was 19th-century French poet, playwright, novelist and critic.

Reineke Hollander is an artist and writer who was born in the Netherlands and has lived in New York City since 1986. She recently finished an autobiographical novel about growing up in the Netherlands after World War II and in the turbulent sixties. Her current concern is how we fail to see "The Other" or "The Others."

Andrew Jarvis is the author of *Sound Points* (Red Bird Press), *Ascent* (Finishing Line Press) and *The Strait* (Homebound Publications). His poems have appeared in *Appalachian Heritage, Evansville Review, Valparaiso Poetry Review, Tulane Review* and many other magazines. He holds an M.A. in writing (poetry) from Johns Hopkins University.

Greg Jenkins is the author of three books and roughly 45 short stories. Among the journals in which his work has appeared are *South Dakota Review, Tampa Review* and *Prairie Schooner.* He has also had a number of plays produced.

Len Krisak's latest books are *The Carmina of Catullus* and *New Poems* of Rilke, both translations. Winner of the Robert Frost and Richard Wilbur awards, he is a four-time champion on *Jeopardy!*

Enid Kassner is a recent graduate of the Johns Hopkins University writing program. Her work has appeared in *Three Quarters Review, Elephant Journal* and other publications. She writes and teaches yoga in Arlington, Virginia.

Christopher Kuhl has been published in *Crack the Spine, Prairie Schooner, Mississippi Literary Review, Piedmont Literary Review* and *Schuylkill Valley Journal of the Arts*, among others. He placed first in the Mississippi Poetry Society competition with his poem "Agon."

John C. Mannone has over 400 works in *Artemis, Southern Poetry Anthology, Still: The Journal, Town Creek Poetry* and others. Author of two poetry collections, he is the poetry editor for *Silver Blade* and *Abyss & Apex.*

Huascar Medina is a former student at Washburn University and the father of a 4-year-old demigod. He is a member of Topeka's Speak Easy Poets group. San Antonio is his hometown, but he doesn't miss things he cannot carry with him. He is also a Magnificent Crow.

Abby Miller grew up in the country around Topeka, Kansas. She was involved in painting and other fine arts from a young age thanks to her local 4-H club. She is now a sophomore at Washburn University and majoring in art with emphasis in painting and drawing.

Kyra Miller lives in Valley Falls and is a senior at Jefferson West High School. She loves to capture the beauty of nature while incorporating unusual, dream-like creatures, ideas, ambiance, and emotions in her work. The ability to create extraordinary things that touch people remains the goal of her work.

Tyler Quintin is an undergraduate working towards his B.F.A. at Washburn University. He is the recipient of the art department's Barbara L. Buzick scholarship, a four-year, full-tuition scholarship awarded to one incoming freshman per year.

Thanks to *Inscape*, **Susan Rich** has now published poems in 49 of the 50 United States. She is author of four collections of poems including *Cloud Pharmacy* and *The Alchemist's Kitchen* and has received awards from the Fulbright Foundation, PEN USA and the *Times Literary Supplement*. She lives in Seattle.

Michael St. Germain is a visual artist and poet obsessed with specificity, reduction and formal constraints. His work is mediated by structure, failure and obfuscation of the past.

M. Trapp teaches literature and writing for UC Berkeley Extension. She writes book reviews for various publications, including *Extract(s)*, *Poetry Northwest*, *Prairie Schooner* and *Terrain*. She has a Ph.D. in English from UC Berkeley, and she is finishing her M.F.A. in writing from Pacific University.

Lee Varon is a writer and social worker. Her work has been nominated for a Pushcart Prize, and she has been published in journals including *Atlanta Review*, *Existere* and *Permafrost*. Her short story "Until the World Brought to Me Again Its Gold Its Vermillion" won the *Briar Cliff Review* Nineteenth Annual Fiction Contest.

Zac Walsh holds a B.A. in philosophy and theology and an M.A. in literature. He is the former editor at large of the *Arroyo Literary Review* and winner of the R.V. Williams Prize for Fiction. He teaches English and passion at Chabot College.

Barbara Waterman-Peters has her studio in the North Topeka Arts District (NOTO). Her award-winning work is in museum and corporate collections and widely shown. Formerly on the faculties of Washburn and Kansas State universities, she devotes herself to painting and writing for *Topeka Magazine.*

Richard K. Weems's first book of stories, *Anything He Wants*, won the Spire Fiction Prize and was a finalist for the Eric Hoffer Book Award. His stories have appeared in *North American Review*, *The Gettysburg Review* and *The Beloit Fiction Journal.*

Dallas Woodburn, a recent Steinbeck Fellow in creative writing, has published fiction and nonfiction in *Fourth River*, *Superstition Review*, *The Nashville Review*, *The Los Angeles Times*, *North Dakota Quarterly*, *Passages North* and *Monkeybicycle*, among others. Her short story collection was a finalist for the Flannery O'Connor Award for Short Fiction and the Horatio Nelson Fiction Prize.

www.ingramcontent.com/pod-product-compliance
Lightning Source LLC
Chambersburg PA
CBHW061108100726
47911CB00012B/454

9780982661772